Dog~of~the~Sea~Waves

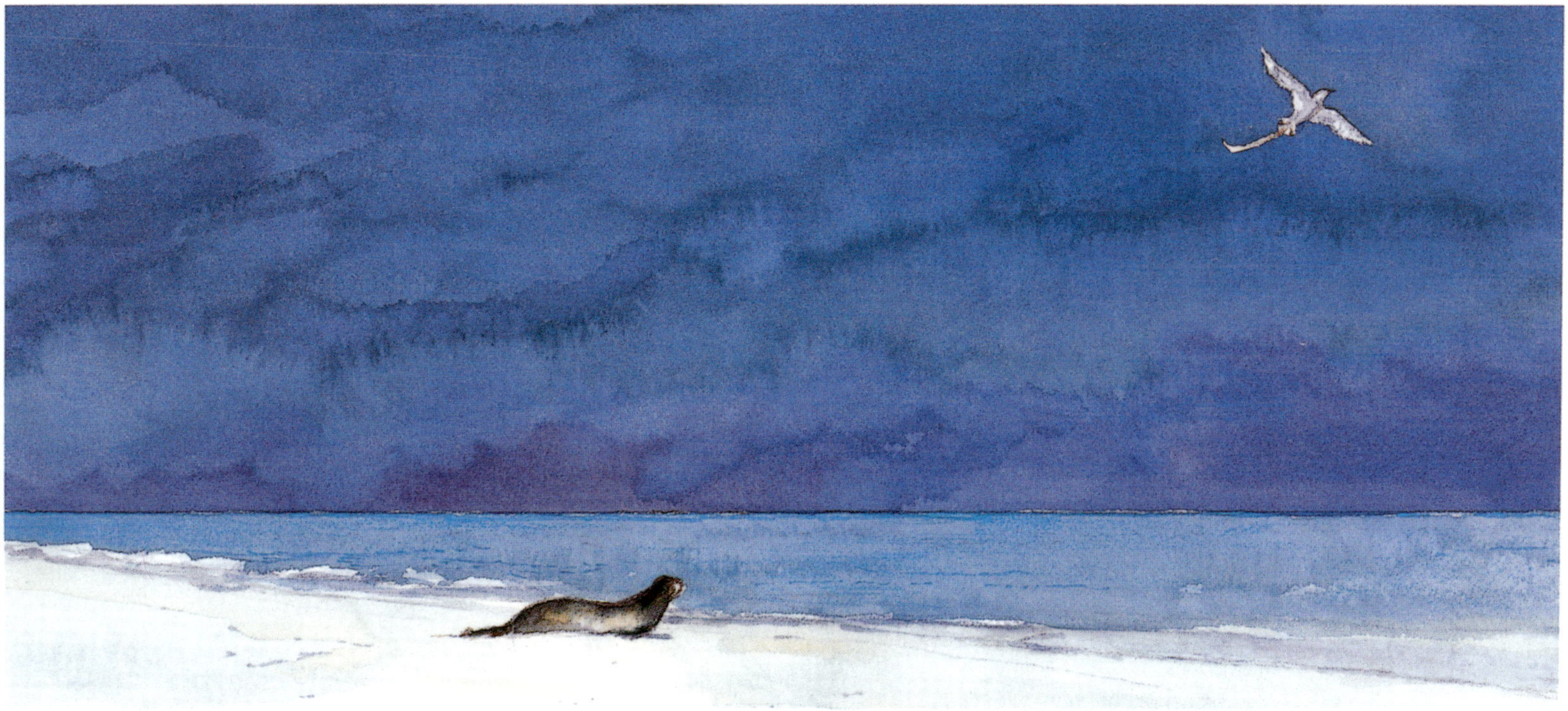

illustrations and story in English & Hawaiian by

James Rumford

McGraw Hill SRA

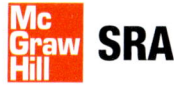

Columbus, OH

DOG-OF-THE-SEA-WAVES, illustrations and story in English and Hawaiian by James Rumford. Copyright © 2004 by James Rumford. Reprinted by permission of Houghton Mifflin Company. All rights reserved.

SRAonline.com

Copyright © 2008 by SRA/McGraw-Hill.

All rights reserved. Except as permitted under the United States Copyright Act, no part of this publication may be reproduced or distributed in any form or by any means, or stored in a database or retrieval system, without the prior written permission of the publisher, unless otherwise indicated.

Printed in Mexico.

Send all inquiries to:
SRA/McGraw-Hill
4400 Easton Commons
Columbus, OH 43219-6188

ISBN 978-0-07-612500-5
MHID 0-07-612500-9

2 3 4 5 6 7 RRM 13 12 11 10 09

The McGraw·Hill Companies

Na Keahiloa Lang

For Leslie Lang

kēia mo'olelo o Hōkū mā

a story of five brothers

i uluhia i ka 'ōlelo kahiko

inspired by the ancient words of the Hawaiian people

a uluhia i ka nani o ka 'āina nei.

and the beauty of this land.

In the days when the sun, the moon, and the stars guided birds with seeds in their bellies to these islands, when ocean waves brought driftwood teeming with life,

Oʻahu Tree Snail

when storms brought

frightened birds in the clouds

and insects on the wind,

the Hawaiian Islands

grew green and lush.

The streams and lagoons

rippled with fish.

Belted Wrasse

And the forests flashed with the feathers of birds and the rainbow wings of insects.

Koa Bug

The Hawaiian Islands welcomed all life that made the long, long journey to its shores, and some two thousand years ago, they embraced the first people to come.

In those days of first canoes, first footprints, first campfires, there were five brothers who came from their home far to the south to explore these islands. They were

    Hōkū, who loved the stars,

    Nāʻale, who loved the sea,

    ʻŌpua, who loved clouds,

    Makani, who loved the wind,

    and Manu, who loved birds.

Kamehameha Butterfly

One night, soon after their arrival, Hōkū said, "See my brothers, that new star I've discovered? It always points north!"

Everyone except Manu looked up at the sparkling North Star. Everyone except Manu began talking excitedly about all the other new things they had discovered.

"New things!" Manu exclaimed. "I miss the old things. Where are the coconuts, the bananas, the sweet potatoes? And how about the pigs, the chickens, the dogs?"

"We'll go home and bring these things back here with us," said Hōkū.

"We're coming back?" Manu cried. "I don't want to come back. I just want to go home."

But home was a long ocean voyage away, and there was much to do before they could leave—food and water to gather and sails to repair. So no one spoke.

The next day, as the brothers were exploring a lagoon, Manu spotted an animal lying at the water's edge.

"It's a dog, my brothers! A dog!"

At last! Something familiar in this strange land.

But when they got close, they saw that it was like no dog they had ever seen before. It had flippers for legs, a fish's tail, and the body of a dolphin. And it was badly hurt.

Manu tried to calm the animal. He brought cool water and cleaned the wound. He built a shelter against the sun and dept the fur wet with seawater.

The brothers left Manu. They had no time for an animal that was going to die. They had to prepare for the long sea voyage home.

Granulated Cowry

But the animal didn't die.

"I will call you 'Dog-of-the-Sea-Waves,' " Manu said on the third day, as he fed him fish.

At the end of the week, the two had their first swim together, and before long, they were playing tag in the waves. Manu made up a silly chant:

> Dog-of-the-Sea-Waves,
> Dog-with-no-paws,
> Dog-with-no-ears,
> Dog-with-no-wag,
> We're friends!

Manu giggled, and Dog-of-the-Sea-Waves tickled his cheek with his whiskers.

Hawaiian Raspberry

"Come help me dry berries and roots for the voyage home," called Hōkū.

"We need fish," scolded Nāʻale.

"There's water to gather," scowled ʻŌpua.

"And sails to repair," cried Makani.

But Manu pretended not to hear. Instead he and Dog-of-the-Sea-Waves played together and got into all kinds of trouble. They terrorized the fish Nāʻale was trying to catch. They made a mess of the beach where Hōkū was drying food. They played with Makani's ropes and accidentally pulled ʻŌpua's gourds off the boat, tripping Makani, who fell into the water.

No one laughed. The two were separated, and Manu was put to work.

Manu gathered berries for Hōkū. He caught fish for Nāʻale. He fetched water for ʻŌpua. He twisted rope for Makani. But every evening after his work was done, he slipped off to meet his friend, and they played in the waves until it got too dark to see. Then Manu swam ashore, and Dog-of-the-Sea-Waves went hunting for food.

After many months of hard work, the boat was finally ready to leave. At the last moment, Manu dived into the water to say goodbye to Dog-of-the-Sea-Waves. As the brothers yelled for Manu to get aboard, Dog-of-the-Sea-Waves brushed his whiskers against Manu's cheek, then disappeared beneath the waves.

The brothers sailed down the island chain. When they came to the last island, 'Ōpua said, "Is that a cloud on the side of that mountain, or smoke? Let's go see."

Curious, the brothers anchored their boat in a quiet bay and swam ashore.

Halfway up the mountain, Makani felt a warm wind and hesitated. But his brothers told him not to worry.

After a few more steps, Manu noticed that the birds were silent. But his brothers paid no attention.

Then — a jolt!

Wēkiu Bug

The earth heaved up and slammed the brothers to the ground. Deep cracks appeared, then flames.

Hōkū grabbed Manu's hand, and the brothers fled down the slope. But a river of fire cut them off from the sea and forced them to the cliffs.

The earth shuddered, and the five brothers jumped — into the sea far below.

But the sea they landed in was a monster.

It thrashed from the earthquakes.

It hissed from the burning lava.

It lashed out at the brothers and grabbed Manu. In an instant, he was gone.

Makani filled his lungs with air and went to the very depths of the ocean, but there was no sign of Manu.

'Ōpua, with his voice like thunder, shouted for Manu above the crashing waves, but there was no answer.

Nā'ale, who loved the sea, begged it to be calm, but it wouldn't listen.

Dragon Moray

All this time, Manu was fighting to get to the surface, but the sea wouldn't let go.

Pompom Crab

Then he felt the whiskers. Manu clasped his arms around Dog-of-the-Sea-Waves, and up they went.

Happyface Spider

It was Hōkū who spotted them. The brothers raced toward Manu and cradled him above the waves.

"Manu, Manu," they cried over and over as they made their way to the boat. And to Dog-of-the-Sea-Waves they chanted their thanks:

>Dog-that-swims-the-depths,
>Dog-that-braves-the-currents,
>Dog-that-knows-the-sea,
>Dog-that-cares-for-our-brother.

The brothers then weighed anchor and headed for the southern sea and home. Manu stood on the deck and listed to Dog-of-the-Sea-Waves barking goodbye.

"We'll be back," Manu shouted.

And when they returned, they came with their families.

They embraced the land and made it their home.

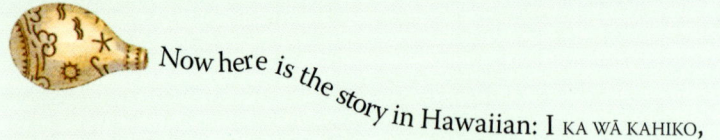

Now here is the story in Hawaiian: I KA WĀ KAHIKO, kuhi ka lā, ka mahina me nā hōkū i ke ala loa i Hawai'i nei. Hiki mai ke kōlea āha'iha'i 'ano'ano. Pae mai ke kāhuli ma ka pīhā. Hao mai ka makani i ka manu o ka wao, i ka pulelehua lahilahi.

Uluwehi a maika'i nā moku. Lapa ke kai i ka 'ōpelu. Lalapa ka wai i ka 'o'opu. Lapalapa ka wao nahele i ka 'ō'ō hinuhinu, i ka pinao ānuenue.

Aloha mai 'o Hawai'i nei i nā mae ola apau i pae a i nā kau iō kikilo loa, apo mai 'o Hawai'i i mā kānaka mua loa.

I kēlā wā o ka wa'a mua loa, o ke kapua'i kanaka, o ke kapuahi kahiko, ua pae mai ka hema mai 'o Fetu'u me kona kaikaina 'ehā: 'O Fetu'u o nā hōkū, 'o Kale o ke kai, 'o Kāpua o nā ao, 'o Matangi o ka makani, 'o Tawake o nā manu.

I kekahi o nā pō ma hope o ia hiki 'ana mai, 'ī mai la 'o Fetu'u, "E ku'u mau kaikaina, e nānā i kēlā hōkū hou. He kūpa'a ia! 'A'ohe like ma ka 'āina o kākou!"

A 'imo'imo ihola ia hōkū kamaha'o 'o Kio-pa'a.

Kikilo a'ela lākou apau iā Kio-pa'a, koe 'o Tawake.

"He aha lā ia mau hōkū iā'u?" i 'uā aku ai 'o Tawake. "Na nā hōkū kākou i alaka'i i kēia 'āina kuānea, tsā!"

A 'ī hou a'ela 'o ia, " 'A'ohe niu a mai'a a uala ma'ane'i. 'A'ohe pua'a . . . moa . . . 'a'ohe 'ilio. 'A'ohe kānaka!"

"E ho'i iho ana i ka hema a e halihali hou mai ana i nā 'ohana o kākou me nā mea apau e pono ai, " mea mai nā kaikua'ana.

"Ho'i mai?" wahi a Tawake. "Makemake au e aku, 'o ia wale!"

A ao, 'oiai lākou e holoholo ana ma ka 'ae one, 'ike akula 'o Tawake aia he holoholona ma ka pili kai.

"He 'ilio! E nā kua'ana! He 'ilio nō!"

Aia kā he mea kama'āina ma kēia moku 'ē!

A 'o ka 'ike pono ihola nō ia he 'ilio nō; 'a'ole na'e ma ke 'ano i 'ike mua 'ia. He hui hono kona wāwae. He pewa i'a kona huelo. He kino naia kona . . . a he 'eha 'ino nō ho'i kona.

Ho'ā'o ihola 'o Tawake e ho'omālie i ia mea. Lawe maila ia i ka wai kai a holoi akula i ka palapū. Kūkulu a'ela 'o ia i ka malumalu nona a ho'opulu mau i kona hulu me ka wai kai.

Ha'alele akula nā kaikau'ana iā Tawake. He ho'opau-manawa wale ka mālama 'ana i kekahi mea e make ana. Pono e ho'omākaukau i ka holomoana.

Eia a'e, 'a'ole kā i make loa ka holoholona.

"E kapa ana au iā'oe he 'Īlio-holo-i-ka-uaua," wahi a Tawake i ke kolu o ka lā, a lawe i wahi i'a nāna.

A hala ke anahulu, 'au'au pū lāua me ke akahele. A pa'ani auane'i lāua i nā'ale. Haku ihola 'o Tawake i wahi mele nona:

'Īlio-holo-i-ka-uaua-o-ka-moana,
'Īlio-hele-i-ka-wāwae'ole,
'Īlio-lohe-i-ka-pepeiao'ole,
'Īlio-ho'okonini-i-ka-huelo'ole,
'O 'oe ho'i hā ku'u 'īlio aloha.

A 'aka'aka a'ela 'o Tawake. Ho'omane'one'o maila 'o 'Īlio-holo-i-ka-uaua i ko Tawake pāpālina me kona mau 'umi'umi.

"E kōkua mai i ke kaula'i," ka 'uā a Fetu'u. "E kōkua mai i ka lawai'a," ke koi a Kale. "E kōkua mai i ke ki'ina wai," ka nuku a Kāpua. "E kōkua mai i ke kāpili pe'a," ke ke'u a Matangi.

Akā ho'okuli akula 'o Tawake a pa'ani kolohe ihola nō lāua. Ho'omaka'u akula lāua i nā i'a. Ho'omōkākī i ke kāhua kaula'i. Pa'ani lāua me nā kaula o ka wa'a. Huki ihola 'o 'Īlio-holo-i-ka-uaua i nā ipu a Kāpua mai luna mai o ka wa'a me ka hili hewa iā Matangi, a hā'ule 'o ia i ke kai.

ʻAʻohe mea ʻakaʻaka, a hoʻokaʻawale ʻia lāua a pono ʻo Tawake e hana. Kōkua ʻo Tawake iā Fetuʻu e ʻimi i ka meaʻai no ka huakaʻi. Lawaiʻa ʻo Tawake me Kale. Kiʻi wai me Kāpua. Wili kaula me Matangi.

Akā, i kēia me kēla ahiahi, hui pū akula ʻo ia me kona hoa, a paʻani ihola lāua. A mōlehulehu, pae maila ʻo Tawake, a holo akula ʻo ʻĪlio-holo-i-ka-uaua i ka ʻimi iʻa.

A pau nā anahulu he nui o ka hana ikaika, ua mākaukau ka waʻa no ka holomoana.

I ka huki ʻana aʻe i ka heleuma, lele ʻōʻō ihola ʻo Tawake ma ke kai a aloha akula ia iā ʻĪlio-holo-i-ka-uaua. A hoʻōho nā kaikuaʻana e eʻe waʻa, hoʻomaneʻoneʻo ʻo ʻĪlio-holo-i-ka-uaua i ko Tawake pāpālina me kona mau ʻumiʻumi, a nalo akula ia ma lalo o nā ʻale.

A kāʻalo ʻo Fatuʻu mā i ka lālani moku, hiki maila lākou i ka moku hope loa, ʻo Hawaiʻi.

"He ao anei, he uahi paha kēla ma uka aku nei?" mea mai ʻo Kāpua. "E piʻi kākou e ʻike."

No laila, kuʻu ihola lākou i ka heleuma, ʻoiai ʻaʻohe wahi e pae ai, a ʻauʻau i ka moku. Iā lākou e piʻi ana i ka mauna, pā maila kekahi makani mehana a kūnānā aʻela ʻo Matangi.

Huli maila ʻo Fetuʻu mā iā ia me ka ʻōlelo, "Mai hopohopo, tsā!" A hoʻomau akula no ka holo ʻana.

Hoʻomaopopo ihola auaneʻi ʻo Tawake i ka mālie loa o nā manu. ʻAʻole naʻe i maliu nā kaikuaʻana. ʻEmo ʻole, he lūlū!

Kū aʻe ka honua a kiola ʻino iā Fetuʻu mā. Wehe a hāmama nā māwae a lapa mai ke ahi. Hopu mai ʻo Fetuʻu i ko Tawake lima a holo heʻe iho lākou apau i kai. A ālai ka pele i ko lākou ala, holo aʻe lākou i ka pali. He lūlū hou, a lele pahū ʻo Fetuʻu mā i ke kai o lalo.

Kohu kupuʻino ka huhū o ke kai. E kūpaka ana nā ʻale i ka ʻōlaʻi a hī ana i ka pele. Hoʻouka ke kai iā Fetuʻu mā. Hao ʻino aku ke kai iā Tawake, a lilo!

Hanu nui ihola ʻo Matangi a luʻu ihola ʻo ia i ka hohonu o ke kai, akā ʻaʻole i ʻike iā Tawake. ʻUā akula ʻo Kāpua me kona leo kohu hekili ma ke kai popoʻi, akā ʻaʻohe pane. Nonoi akula ʻo Kale, nānā i aloha i ke kai, i nā nalu e mālie iho, akā ʻaʻole i hoʻokō ia.

I ia wā nō, paio akula ʻo Tawake e ea aʻe i ka ʻilikai, akā, hoʻopaʻa ā paʻa ke kai iā ia. A laila, pā lihi ma kona pāpālina nā ʻumiʻumi o kona hoa. Pūʻili akula ia iā ʻĪlio-holo-i-ka-uaua, a ea aʻela lāua.

Na Fetuʻu lāua i ʻike mua. ʻAuʻau akula nā kaikuaʻana iō Tawake, a hāpai aʻela lākou iā ia ma luna o nā ʻale. "Auē, e Tawake! Auē, e Tawake ē!" i ʻuē mai ai lākou, ʻoiai lākou e ʻauʻau ana i ka waʻa.

A laila mahalo maila lākou iā ʻĪlio-holo-i-ka-uaua me ke mele penei:

ʻĪlio-holo-i-ke-kai-hohonu,
ʻĪlio-ʻaʻa-i-ke-kai-kuolo,
ʻĪlio-ʻike-i-nā-kai-ʻewalu,
ʻĪlio-mālama-iā-Tawake lā!

Huki aʻela ʻo Fetuʻu mā i ka heleuma a huli akula lākou i ka ʻāina o lākou ma ka hema. Ua kū ʻo Tawake ma ka pola ʻoiai e emō aku ana ʻo ʻĪlio-holo-i-ka-uaua i kona aloha aku. "E hoʻi ana nō mākou," i ʻuā mai ai ʻo Tawake.

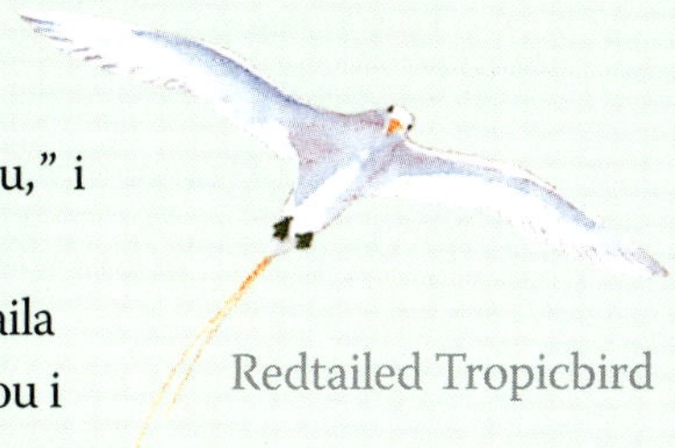

A iā lākou i hoʻi mai ai, hele pū maila me nā ʻohana o lākou. A pili paʻa lākou i ka ʻāina, a lilo ʻo Hawaiʻi nei i ēwe ʻāina no lākou. PAU

Redtailed Tropicbird

37

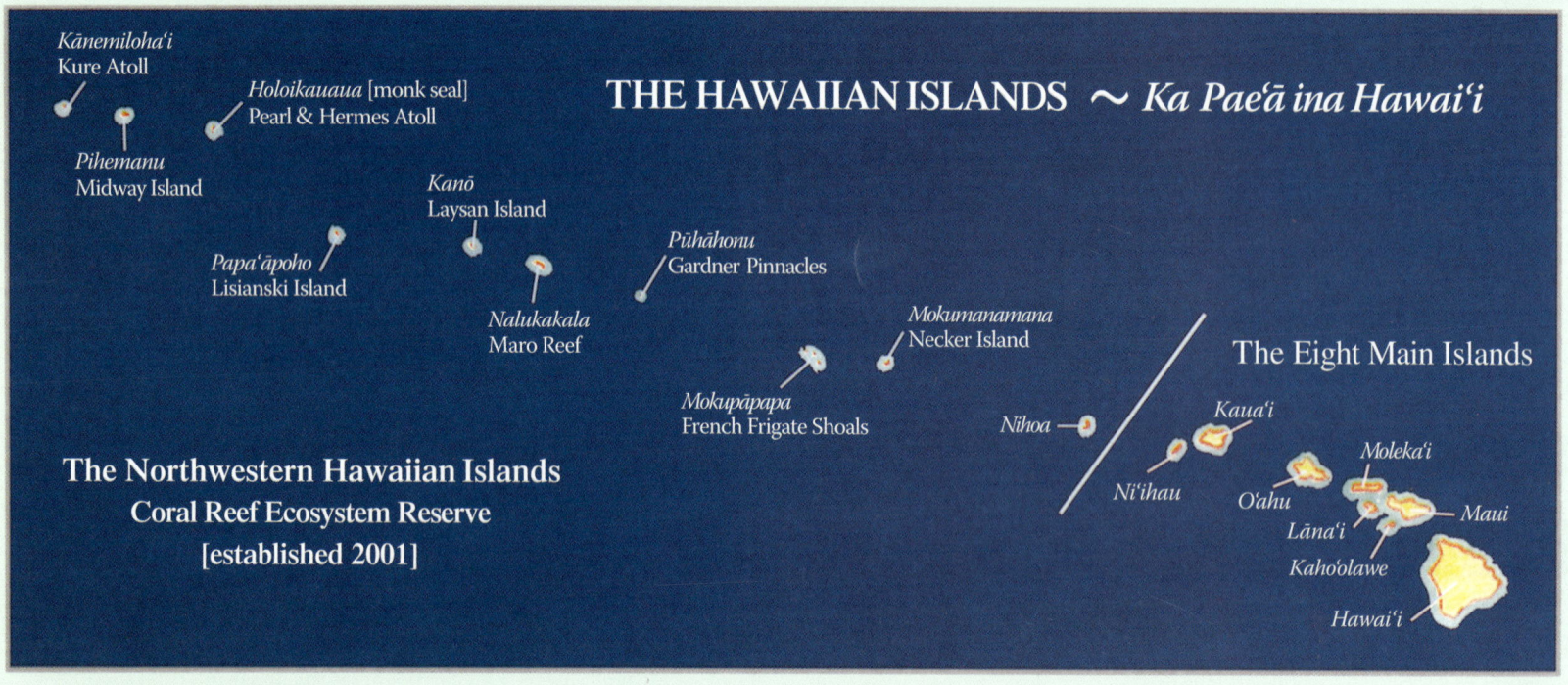

Hawai'i is one of the most isolated regions in the world. Much of the life that evolved in the island chain exists nowhere else.

How did life get to Hawai'i? By wind and wave. But the process was slow. Only once every 40,000 years or so was the journey successful. Most of the time, life perished in the vast sea separating the islands from the rest of the world.

By far, nature's most successful transporter has been man, who has brought thousands of new species. These new species are taking over the land. The ecosystem that took millions of years to form has all but collapsed. Unable to compete, many native plants and animals have perished and many more are near extinction.

Man now has a new role. He must learn to protect the environment. He must learn to preserve Hawai'i's unique life forms. He must learn *aloha 'āina* to cherish these special islands.

When the first people arrived in the Hawaiian islands some two thousand years ago, they saw a very different land from the one we see today. I have tried to imagine what Hawai'i looked like then in my paintings. In these paintings and scattered throughout the book, you will find some of the plants and animals that the first people saw. Many of these life forms are found only in Hawai'i. On the following pages is a brief description of each plant and animal. Those that are unique are marked with a sea urchin design, . Many are endangered. These are marked with waves, . Some, like the *'ō'ō'ā'ā* bird, haven't been seen in twenty years. All are in need of our care and protection.

Pronounce the Hawaiian *a, e, i, o, u* something like *ah, ay, ee, oh, oo*. Lengthen vowels marked with a *kahakō* [¯] and keep vowels apart that are separated by the Hawaiian letter ['], called *'okina*. *W* is sometimes pronounced *v*. In the following examples the bold letters show the accented syllables: Hawai'i [huh-*vai* ee], Nā'ale [*nah* ah-lay], 'Ōpua [oh-*poo*-wah], '*ō' ō' ā' ā* [oh oh ah ah], 'ilioholoikauaua [ee-lee-yo-ho-lo-yi-kuh-*wa*-wa], 'i'iwi [ee ee-vee], wēkiu [*way-kee*-yoo].

Hawaiian Monk Seal
Monachus schauinslandi

Although the monk seal lives in the uninhabited northwestern chain, you might see one resting on the beach on one of the eight main islands, where people live. If you do, keep a safe distance. Unlike Dog-of-the-Sea-Waves, a monk seal can be dangerous, especially if wounded. The Hawaiian word for the monk seal is ʻilioholoikauaua or "the ʻilio that rides the rough [seas]." An ʻilio is a dog, but it once meant any strange furry animal. The seal was strange to the early Hawaiians because they had only dogs, pigs, and rats, all three of which they brought to these islands. There are about 1,400 seals left in the entire island chain. [page 1]

Redtailed Tropicbird
Phaeton rubicauda

The redtailed tropicbird is a flying acrobat. It plays in the warm air currents and looks magnificent with its two red tail feathers. It flies over the ocean looking for squid and fish. When it spots its prey, it plunges into the water with lightning speed. In Hawaiian the tropicbird is called koeʻe. In this story it is the symbol of Manu, and in the Hawaiian version Manu is called Tawake, the ancient Polynesian form for koeʻe. [page 37]

Oʻahu Tree Snail
Achatinella apexfulva

Tree snails are called pūpū. They are about three quarters of an inch long. They live inside beautiful striped shells. You can find them asleep under leaves in forests high in the mountains. They wake up at night to feed on fungi. Tree snails came to Hawaiʻi several million years ago. Slowly they spread over all the islands until each island— in fact, each valley— seemed to have its own kind of tree snail. [page 5]

Fan Palm
Pritchardia beccariana

When you think of Hawaiʻi, you think of coconut palms. But Hawaiʻi had no coconut palms before the Polynesians brought them. Instead the islands were covered with forests of fan palms. Today these forests are gone. Early Hawaiians cut the forests down for building materials. Pigs, rats, and goats ate the seedlings and the seeds. Some species have only a few trees left. [page 6]

Kauaʻi Black Honey Eater
Moho braccatus

No one has seen this bird, the ʻōʻōʻāʻā, nor heard its flutelike call, since the 1980's. If the ʻōʻōʻāʻā is not extinct, it is flying about the Alakaʻi Swamp on the island of Kauaʻi, feeding on its favorite blossoms. [page 6]

Belted Wrasse
Stethojulis balteata

You can see this six-inch-long belted wrasse or ʻōmaka darting around the reefs close to shore. If the ʻōmaka sees you, it will disappear beneath the sand. [page 7]

Koa Bug
Coleotichus blackburniæ

You can sometimes find this puʻu, or bug, feeding on the native koa tree (*Acacia koa*). The koa bug was once common, but certain flies and wasps, brought to Hawaiʻi in the twentieth century, attack and kill the koa bug. Defenseless, the koa bug is starting to disappear. [page 8]

Kamehameha Butterfly
Vanessa tameamea

This butterfly was named for the first king of the Hawaiian Islands, Kamehameha I (?1758–1819). The Hawaiians call this butterfly pulelehua. Pulelehua are rare, but you might see one along the bank of a stream far from people. What you probably won't see are the caterpillars and the cocoons. They are too well camouflaged. [page 10]

Hawaiian Goose
Branta sandvicensis

The nene or Hawaiian goose is the official state bird of Hawaiʻi. Once it was hunted for food, and fifty years ago there were only thirty birds left. Today there are more than eight hundred Hawaiian geese in the wild, thanks to the people who worked hard to protect them. [page 10]

Hawaiian Honey Creeper
Vestiaria coccinea

The Hawaiians call this bird ʻiʻiwi. If you climb up to the forests on Maui, Kauaʻi, or Hawaiʻi above 2,000 feet, you may see the ʻiʻiwi in the tallest trees. Listen for its call. It sounds like a rusty hinge. [page 11]

Yellow Hibiscus
Hibiscus brackenridgei

This is the official state flower of Hawaiʻi and is called maʻo hau hele or pua aloalo. It grows in dry forests and shrublands. Newly arrived plants and animals threaten the maʻo hau hele. Today the flower is disappearing in the wild. Soon you may see it only in gardens. [page 14]

Granulated Cowry
Cypræa granulata

There are several varieties of leho or cowries found only in Hawaiʻi. Some are rare. The granulated cowry or leho pupuʻu is one such Hawaiian cowry. It is about an inch long and lives in tide pools and in water up to sixty feet deep. [page 15]

Milletseed Butterflyfish
Chætodon miliaris

This fish has a beautiful Hawaiian name, lauwiliwili. It makes me think of golden-colored leaves *(lau)* turning and twisting *(wiliwili)* in the wind. This six-inch-long fish lives in the reef and is very curious. If you are snorkeling, it will come up to you to find out what you are doing. [page 17]

39

Hawaiian Raspberry
Rubus hawaiiensis

The Hawaiian raspberry grows in wet forests in the mountains and has no thorns, unlike its cousins in other parts of the world. The Hawaiian raspberry is called *'akala*, which is also the word for "pink." [page 19] ☼

Hawaiian Hoary Bat
Lasiurus cinereus semotus

Before the Polynesians came, the hoary bat was the only land mammal to make it to these islands. The Hawaiian word for this bat is *pe'a* or *'ōpe'ape'a*. The word *pe'a* reminds us how beautiful this animal is in flight, for the word also means "a kite" or "a sail." The hoary bat sleeps in the day and hunts for insects at night. [page 20] ≈≈≈

Hawaiian Hawk
Buteo solitarius

The *'io* or Hawaiian hawk is endangered but is slowly making a comeback. There are now about 2,500 birds. The *'io* builds its nests in native forests. It eats whatever small animal or insect it can catch in its sharp claws. It is a majestic bird and was once a symbol of royalty. And when it cries, it says its Hawaiian name, "ee-oh." [page 22] ☼ ≈≈≈

'Ama'u Fern
Sadleria cyantheoides

The *'ama'u* fern is amazing. No sooner does the lava cool than the wind brings *'ama'u* spores to colonize the new land. The young ferns sprout up red like molten lava. The older ones turn a cool shade of green. And if the climate is right, within time the *'ama'u* fern will help turn the barren lava into a forest of ferns and trees. [page 23] ☼

Wēkiu Bug
Nysius wekiuicola

You would have to climb the tallest mountain in the world to see this tiny insect one fourth of an inch long. It lives near the *wekiu* or summit of the volcano Mauna Kea, which rises 33,482 feet above the ocean floor. The *Wekiu* can't fly but has long enough legs to scurry over the lava to catch other insects that the wind has carried up the slopes of the mountain. Because it is so cold where it lives, the *wekiu* has a special chemical in its blood to keep it from freezing. [page 23] ☼

Dragon Moray
Enchelycore pardalis

There are many kinds of eels or *puhi* that make Hawai'i their home. The dragon moray with its long nose tubes, sharp teeth, and bright spots looks dangerous, and it is, if bothered. It is about three feet long and prefers to live in the Northwestern Hawaiian Islands. [page 27] ☼

Pompom Crab
Lybia edmondsoni

This tiny crab called *kūmimi pua* holds two stinging anemones in its claws. The anemones help the crab chase away enemies. In return for this help, the crab lets the anemones eat the leftovers from the meals it catches. Scuba divers have to go down about sixty feet to see this crab. [page 28] ☼

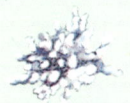

Finger Coral
Porites compressa

Corals were one of the most important animals to come to Hawai'i. They formed the reefs that protected the shoreline from giant waves and provided homes for thousands of sea plants and animals. The reefs also formed the beaches as the waves broke up the coral that had died and washed it to shore as sand. Finger coral is called *pōhaku puna*, or "coral stone" in Hawaiian, and grows in areas protected from waves. It can live close to shore or in water as deep as 150 feet. [page 28] ☼

Happyface Spider
Theridon grallator

This spider's body is only one fourth of an inch long. It has many different markings on its back, and sometimes they look like a happy face. That is what William Mull thought in 1972 when he coined the name for the spider. In Hawaiian, the spider is called *nananana makaki'i*, or "the masked spider." The happyface spider lives in the native forest about 2,000 to 4,000 feet above sea level. [page 30] ☼

Use the scientific name to search the Internet for more information about each plant and animal. Two excellent books are *Remains of a Rainbow* by D. Littschwager and S. Middleton and the third edition of *Atlas of Hawai'i*.

KEY

☼ = *the species is endemic*

≈≈≈ = *the species is endangered*

40